THE
DEEPER LIFE

AN INTRODUCTION TO
CHRISTIAN MYSTICISM

by Louis Dupré

CROSSROAD • NEW YORK

1981
The Crossroad Publishing Company
575 Lexington Avenue,
New York, NY 10022

Printed in the United States of America

Library of Congress Cataloging in Publication Data

Dupré, Louis K.
The deeper life.

1. Mysticism—Addresses, essays, lectures.   I. Title.
BV5082.2.D86   248.2'2   81–3275
ISBN   0–8245–0007–5 (pbk.)   AACR2

The Deeper Life

Contents

Preface

When I finished reading *The Deeper Life*, I realized that I had read a book written with love. For many years I have admired Louis Dupré and his work. As a colleague at Yale University, I have come to know him as an erudite scholar, an inspiring teacher, and a faithful friend. But when I went through the chapters of this book, I noticed something that his earlier work had not shown. I felt a deep spiritual affection undergirding the sentences, an affection that binds the reader to the subject in a unique way.

In this small volume Louis Dupré not only writes clearly and intelligently about the richness and complexity of the mystical life, but he also communicates in a very personal way that he himself and we, his readers, can live this life. He not only wants to analyze and clarify the mysterious ways of the Divine Spirit, but he also wants to convince us that we can experience that same Spirit in the midst of our daily joys and sorrows. He not only wants to explain the different mystical ways, but he also wants to encourage us to recognize them in our own struggles. He not only wants to be an instructor, but also a comforter. That is what makes this book such a treasure for the reader.

While reading, I remained constantly aware that these words were first spoken to the Trappist monks at the Abbey of Gethsemani in Kentucky. I kept hearing Louis' inspired voice in this—for him so unusual—milieu, and I kept seeing eager faces listening to this—for them so unusual—visitor. And I was drawn into the mutual recognition that the presence which was spoken about had become tangible in this unusual encounter itself.

Different powerful sentences kept leaping up: "Christian mystics never advocate the choice of suffering for its own sake, but always for the love of the suffering Christ. . . . To the Christian Christ presents the perfect creature, the only one he or she may hope to love as God loves the creature. . . . Christianity, whatever we may think of its historical record, has taught people to love. . . . Suffering alone, if freely accepted, safeguards love against selfishness. . . . The broken self appears to be the only self worth giving. . . . Christian piety teaches that every suffering of mine, however despicable and even sinful in its origin, is Jesus' agony in me. . . . What mostly distinguishes the mystic from the ordinary person is his or her willingness to regard suffering, even in its most humiliating aspects, as a most individual vocation. . . . If grace is not the exclusive privilege of a few, then neither is the experience of grace."

These and many other words were much more than words to me. They were events. Truth was happening. A truth not just for monks but for all people. Indeed, there is no special truth for monks because what is most true for them is most true for all who live outside the walls of their monasteries.

I am filled with gratitude by the awareness that these words, brought with love to the monastery, are now brought from there to all who want to hear them in their innermost being.

HENRI J.M. NOUWEN

Foreword

The following pages contain the text of nine lectures I gave to the monks of Gethsemani Abbey in Kentucky. I never intended to publish what I had not "written." Yet after the tapes and even some partial transcription had circulated among monasteries for five years, Richard Payne, the Editorial Director of The Crossroad Publishing Company, requested me to "do something" with them. I hesitated but let myself be persuaded that the spontaneity of a spoken, and often improvised, address would compensate for its lack of polish. So I edited the transcript but did not rewrite it. Needless to say, the present text can claim neither scholarly merit nor literary grace. I shall be happy if it would allow a few readers to share the feeling of wonder and spiritual excitement aroused by our participation in that most daring adventure of the Christian mind: its mystical quest of God.

With gratitude and affection, I now return this humble report of our common journey to my fellow travellers, the monks of Gethsemani.

Louis Dupré

Introduction

What business do I, a worldly man mainly acquainted with modern philosophy and Marxist theory, have speaking to you about mysticism? However I attempt to justify my assumed task, spiritual authority does definitely not enter into its justification. For my speaking is motivated by poverty and want, rather than by riches and abundance. In the end this negative motivation may be as good as any. In the kingdom of God there are no possessors—only beggars. Even the elementary rule of human prudence does not apply: Of that which we know not we must remain silent. Of God no one "knows" and so it must be desire rather than possession that urges us to speak.

Nevertheless in one modest sense we all know something of an experience which is not in all respects the exclusive privilege of a few. How well I remember the pleasant surprise with which I heard, many years ago, an old and saintly Jesuit, a specialist in medieval spirituality, introduce his lectures on mystical theology: "You are all well acquainted with what I am going to discuss." Of course, we do not all move on the same spiritual level. Nor can anyone reach by his own efforts that height of spiritual awareness for which we should reserve the term "mystical." But our own experiences of the mysterious presence of Christmas night, of the inexplicable joy of Easter morning, of the inner silence of solitary prayer, modest as they are, remain nevertheless fully continuous with those of the masters of spiritual life.

The need out of which I speak is not merely personal; it is the need of an entire age that has lost the direct presence of the sacred and that has replaced transcendence by self-transcending. We may call the prevailing climate a-theistic, not because faith has disappeared in our time, but because the question whether we believe in God or not, retains little or no practical bearing upon our lives. Braving this hostile climate the believer carefully nurtures the flame of a secret faith—secret not because he has to hide it, but because it has become hidden by its total incongruity with a radically secular environment. Even to the believer himself the flame of his faith has become secret, since it no longer enlightens his whole life. He remains as much in the dark, as much caught up in the swirl of a secular existence, as the unbeliever. And when occasionally he retires to that inner sanctuary of his faith, he spends most of his time waiting—*waiting in expectation.* No age, then, seems more removed from mystical fervor than our own. And yet none comes closer to it in spiritual need. Our very poverty is our wealth. The night is our light. For the desert of God's absence is an emptiness that, in the believer, longs for total fulfilment. Only in the mystic's dark night does the contemporary seeker of God recognize a spiritual similarity to his own religious condition: here at least God is present through his felt absence. Men and women of our time, however confused in religious matters, have not been mistaken in detecting a kinship with those who appear to be farthest removed from them. Hence they have turned to the mystics, rather than to the moralists or the theologians, for enlightenment.

The Deeper Life

·1·

The Word and
the Experience

The early Fathers applied the term *mystical* to the reading of Scripture insofar as the Gospel of Christ reveals a deeper meaning in the Old Testament text. This "mystical" reading of the Scriptures was in no way private or secret since it was open to every Christian believer. Eventually the biblical meaning led to a sacramental one. Even as Christ is hidden in the Scriptures, so is he hidden in the Eucharist. Hence, the mystical element came to refer to the sacramental symbol. But one meaning complements the other. For Origen the Christian has access to a mystical (i.e., experiential) knowledge of God both by reading the Scriptures and by receiving the sacraments. Never, in the patristic period, did the term mystical refer to a purely subjective, private experience. Experience it was, but the experience of the entire Christian community. The Eastern Church has preserved this communal sense of the term even today.

From this older Christian usage we retain the notion that the experience of God's grace is, to a greater or lesser degree, available to each Christian, in and through his union with the Church and, through the Church, with God. We have onesidedly replaced this communal meaning of the *divina pati* by that of a private experience. In doing so we have not only privatized what was in the beginning viewed as a *shared* experience, but perhaps also unduly separated experience from all other aspects of religion. Religion is, of course, never pure experience, least of all purely subjective experience. It is always primarily a response to a calling. To the extent that that response is active, we call it an attitude. But this active response would not have been given if some part of ourselves didn't resonate to the transcendent appeal. Without some kind of preliminary, passively infused experience few would ever freely adopt a religious attitude and none would do so with the inspiration and devotion characteristic of true religion. Mysticism in the widest sense, understood as some passively infused experience, belongs to the core of all religious faith, whether communal or private.

Before entering upon the discussion of this passive religious experience, we must pause to consider another, more comprehensive definition of mysticism, current today, which is by no means restricted to the religious experience. According to that modern definition, mysticism consists in an expansion of the conscious self beyond its ordinary boundaries to a point where it achieves a union with a "greater" reality. The experience is accompanied by a new feeling of integration, both with oneself and with that reality. Thus we speak of "nature mysticism" when the self expands into such a union with its physical environment. Some of you are undoubtedly acquainted with the beautiful descriptions of such states in Richard Jeffries' *The Story of My Heart*. Allow me to quote one at random here:

> I was utterly alone with the sun and the earth. Lying down on the grass, I spoke in my soul to the earth, the sun, the air and the distant sea far beyond sight. I thought of the earth's firmness—I felt it bear me up; through the grassy couch there came an influence as if I could feel the great earth speaking to me. I thought of the wandering air—its pureness, which is its beauty. The air touched me and gave me something of itself. I spoke to the sea . . . green at the rim of the earth and blue in deeper ocean; I desired to have its strength, its mystery and glory. Then, I addressed the sun, desiring the soul equivalent of his light and brilliance, his endurance and unwearied race. I turned to the blue heaven over, gazing into its depths, inhaling its exquisite color and sweetness. The rich blue of the unattainable flower of the sky drew my soul towards it, and there it rested, for pure color is rest of heart. By all these, I prayed; I felt an emotion of the soul beyond all definition. Prayer is a puny thing to it and the word is a rude sign to the feeling, but I know no other.[1]

It is not easy to do justice to this beautiful passage. I used to think that it expressed a nonreligious, mystical experience. But I am no longer sure that the characteristically religious awareness of distance or, if you allow me to use the technical term, *permanent transcendence*, is absent from the experience. Even while the writer merges with nature to an unprecedented state of union, he nevertheless appears to preserve an awareness that he is allowed to partake in what infinitely and lastingly *surpasses* himself. This awareness of distance, rather than the name of the mystical reality (whether it be God or "nature") is, I believe, what distinguishes religious from nonreligious mysticism. Jeffries' description evokes a host of others, some equally ambiguous (I think of Wordsworth's "Tintern Abbey"), others clearly nonreligious (some of Albert Camus' early Algerian sketches appear to have been inspired by a feeling of mystical merging with the sea, the sun, and the sand). There is enough evidence to support calling some experiences mystical, though not obviously, or though obviously not, religious. Nor is all nonreligious mysticism necessarily of the extrovert type: there exists an introvert turning of the self into itself that admits no transcendence of a deeper self, an Atman, but that achieves a new integration within the individual self. I suspect that some forms of yoga, as they are practiced today, may belong to this variety. Can we still speak of "expansion" in the case of such a self-enclosed self? Obviously not in the outward-oriented sense, but that is not the only possible meaning of the "expansion" of consciousness. For here the self expands *within itself* and thereby achieves a wholly new state of consciousness. At any rate, it is not this nonreligious mysticism I wish to discuss. There is also a religious mysticism of the self. To this I now turn.

·2·

The Way Inward

The mysticism of the self has been articulated with classical precision in the Upanishads and the later Vedantic commentaries, especially those of the eighth-century Indian sage, Shankara. To dismiss it as nonreligious because of its discrepancy with native Western mysticism would show considerable cultural bias. Indeed, for all its intrinsic limitations this mysticism of the deeper self may well provide the best introduction to a spiritual understanding of man. I became interested in its underlying concept of man after having worked my way through a sizable amount of Marxist literature. All of this literature starts from the basic assumption that the human person constantly surpasses himself in being always on the way to an ideal that goes beyond the present reality. What I did not find in Marx, and what nevertheless struck me as being equally significant, is that this process of transcendence occurs passively as well as actively. The person is attracted by an ideal that surpasses not merely his present achievement, but even his future potential. And, most importantly, that ideal *affects his present reality.* Beyond his ordinary self he finds a deeper Being that he cannot actively control, that in some mysterious manner forms the ground of himself. About that inward self Indian mystics have spoken with great wisdom and insight. It is also an essential, though often neglected part of Christian mysticism. For the mystical consciousness, at least implicitly, assumes that, underneath the familiar succession of sensations and reflections, a more permanent self rests in which space and time are transformed into vistas of an inner realm with its own rhythms and perspectives. Full self-knowledge must reach to that deeper dimension hidden below the ordinary consciousness with which we work, talk, and study. All around our rational consciousness, William James claimed, and separated from it by the flimsiest of screens, there are potential forms of consciousness of a completely different nature. To this deeper self the mystical experience gives access.

For the Christian it is the point where God and the soul touch, the divine basis on which human selfhood rests. It is what Tauler called "the ground of the soul" and Eckhart "the little castle." Catherine of Siena speaks of the "interior home of the heart," Teresa of the "inner castle" and John of the Cross of the "house at rest . . . in darkness and concealment." All these metaphors suggest a secret dwelling where God resides, the center of my created being which remains permanently united with God's creative act. In Michelangelo's fresco on the vault of the Sistine Chapel Adam's outstretched hand has just been released from the divine finger, and an empty space has begun to separate the two. The mystic knows that the hand and the finger continue to touch in a common space. That space is the deeper self, the sanctuary without images, as Plotinus called it.

Thus while thinking only about God the Christian

mystic teaches an important lesson about the self, namely, that self is in its deepest nature more than itself. To move into myself means in the end to move beyond myself into what is "higher" than the self or "deeper" than the self. The mystic knows all the time that man is that particular being that is *more than man*. In the language of modern philosophy, the person is a self-transcending being, yet not merely, or even mainly, through what he *does* but through what he *is* in his very nature.

Precisely because God dwells first and foremost in the self, the mystical journey is mostly an inward journey. Our own Christian tradition has always taught that the gate that gives access to the inner land is *memory*. In English we refer to the religious way of remembering by the beautiful word *recollection*. A most appropriate term. Not only do I reverse the forward-and-outward movement of ordinary consciousness toward the inward *source* of my active life, but in doing so I re-collect myself out of the constant dispersion of time. The way back into the past is the inward way, the way to togetherness. The root of the Germanic term for memory is *inner* (*Erinnerung, herinnering, erindring*). Recollection means, indeed, far more than recall: it is interiorization.

Now, in a very real sense, all spiritual life consists in a constant "rereading" of oneself and, beyond that self, of all history. It attempts to review the temporal succession of my existence in its totality and thereby to grasp it in its unity. To succeed in this task it must move in the direction of the primeval nothingness, the point of simple unity in which my existence took its origin. There where I was acted upon before I started acting, I expect to feel the eternal presence, what St. John of the Cross called "the substantial touch." Through the gate of memory I travel to the inner land where the core of my existence may be revealed. To know oneself religiously is to remember one's origin, to move to one's source. Here the deepest immanence of being with myself becomes the highest transcendence of being with God.

Christian mystics have always assigned a special place to memory in the dispensation of spiritual life. When the soul withdraws to a level where the other faculties no longer operate, memory still functions. According to Saint Teresa, memory remains active in the state of quiet long after the soul has lost control over thinking and willing. It is, of course, Saint Augustine who has, in a definitive way, drawn attention to the religious significance of memory. In the Tenth Book of his *Confessions* he raises the question: "But where in my memory do You abide, Lord? Where in my memory do You abide? What resting place have You claimed as your own? What sanctuary built for Yourself? You have paid this honor to my memory, that You deign to abide in it, but I now come to consider in what *part* of it You abide . . . . In recalling You to mind, I have mounted beyond those parts of memory which I have in common with the animals, and . . . I did not find You among the images of corporeal beings."[1]

Indeed, for spiritual life it is not sufficient to remember events. Recalling the past can paralyze the powers that enable us to act in the present and to plan for the future. A past thus remembered, far from opening onto a deeper self, merely inhibits the functioning of the ordinary self. This is the kind of remembrance to which Kierkegaard referred when he wrote, "The worst thing for me is to remember. The moment I remember a life relationship it loses its actuality." These words reflect his own inability to live in the immediate reality, an inability which eventually forced him to break his engagement to the woman he loved. We recognize the same tendency to view the present only through the reflection of the past in Rousseau's claim that things became true to him only when he remembered them. In such instances a romantic fascination, or pathological obsession, with the past, allows the reflective attitude to dominate all of existence to the point where we view the present only through the eyes of the past. Alain Renais' film "Last Year in Marienbad" has given a poetic expression to a consciousness reduced to memory which carries the present over into the past.

Still, Augustine insists, God resides in my memory. "And yet, You deign to dwell in my memory ever since the time I first learned of you." He does not say *how* God inhabits memory, but he shows how only the recollection that moves inward encounters God in the mind. "For behold, you were within me and I outside." But how is it that memory gives access to the inner self? Clearly no accumulation of memories will ever open the inner gate. The purpose is not to recall as much of my past as possible, but, as in the psychoanalytic process, to integrate the multiplicity of that past within a new, unifying pattern and to discover a different structure that changes my perspective upon myself. To remember myself religiously is to recollect my total existence, beyond actual remembrances, by descending, along the ladder of memories, into the very ground of my being. Thus in remembering my past I travel back into the vacuum of my original nothingness, and beyond, into the source of my existence. If time is a constant flight from my origin, recollection returns me to it.

True recollection leads to *confession*. In the recollection of his *Soliloquies* St. Augustine reviews his past life before God, but only in the *Confessions* does he *fully* remember his life, that is, not only as he has actively lived it, but as he has received it. Here his autobiography turns into confession. Now confession has a connotation of guilt and sinfulness. To know my past in its entirety is to know myself as guilty. Who can remember himself before God without remembering how he abused the divine gift? A past fully remembered is a guilty past. To be present to oneself is to be present to oneself as good, yes, but also as evil. That is why Kierkegaard says, "I can choose myself truly only in repentance." Only in repentance do I accept evil as an essential part of my past and at the same time repent it, repudiate it, as an estrangement of my real self. To accept myself is to choose myself in repentance. Of course, in itself guilt is neither religious nor redemptive. But *accepted* guilt forms an essential part of that memory which leads us inwardly. Only when I am able to confess do I admit my real past with its failings before God. I must accept my guilt, a task so painful that it deters most people. Temple Drake, the heroine of William Faulkner's play, *Requiem for a Nun*, is unable to confess her guilt in the death of her child. She desperately moves between the sinful past that she has become, and her present desire to be cleansed. The future is closed to her, because she cannot bring herself to confess. Recollecting one's whole past in confession leads to the entrance to the interior life, the beginning of an inward journey beyond the self.

It is not the self as such that the religious person seeks, but what is revealed in and through that self. Even those Indian mystics who speak exclusively about the self, the Atman, do not refer to a self-conscious subject, but to a deeper reality in which thinking and being are one. Hence being itself becomes conscious, and consciousness becomes being. The substance of the soul which God "touches" is clearly more than the individual self of which I am fully conscious. In one sense the paradox of the Mandukhya Upanishad is literally true: it is a state of consciousness that lies beyond dreamless sleep. Buddhism shows a similar concern in emphasizing the need for overcoming individual personhood. From a religious viewpoint the individual self is not an ultimate. The soul is called to move beyond self-consciousness in that deeper realm upon which individual selfhood rests.

·3·

God:
Being and Manifestation

The mystical path of the West differs from that of the East. Yet what distinguishes them is the *approach* to the Absolute, not, or not primarily, the nature of the Absolute. Easterners tend to look inward, while Westerners look mostly either at the cosmos or to the person for an encounter with the transcendent. It would, of course, be simplistic to classify all Hindu or Buddhist mysticism as introspective, and all Jewish and Christian as cosmic or interpersonal. Augustine and many who followed him turned their glance inward while Zen Buddhists adopt the kind of total openness toward the external world which is the ultimate objectivity. Nevertheless, opposite tendencies exist and they are nowhere more evident than among those Christian mystics who share the Eastern reluctance to give names to the Absolute.

Negative theology, as we call the mystical ascent that leaves all creaturely names behind, has assumed a new significance in an age when discourse about God has lost much of its past authority. To many of our contemporaries also the traditional attributes have become questionable and even the divine name has become desecrated by centuries of profanating controversy. Still they continue to experience the need to move beyond all finite reality to a henceforth nameless ultimate. The Christian tradition itself initiated its mystical quest by emphasizing the difference between the God we seek and the human predicates by which we name Him. The mysterious sixth-century monk to whom we now refer as Pseudo-Dionysius offered a description that became a spiritual program for many later mystics. "In the earnest exercise of mystical contemplation abandon all sensation and intellection and all objects or sensed or seen and all being and all nonbeing and in unknowing, as much as may be, be one with the beyond being and knowing."[1]

If consistently maintained, such extreme negations would result in a divine darkness that excludes any kind of divine revelation. But for Christian mystics the negation of divine names has been a method of spiritual ascent more than a theoretical principle. Negative theology has always recognized that God is *manifest*, even though none of our attributes adequately describe Him. In the end the dark of unknowing turns into the light of divine self-manifestation. What distinguishes its spiritual ascent is that the divine unity constitutes a point of ultimate rest. Other Christian mystics move out of this resting place again into the works of God's self-manifestation in a continuous rhythm of expansion and contraction, work and rest, manifestation and recollection. This seemingly abstract distinction has significant spiritual consequences. For it determines the mystic's ability to take part in the communication of the divine "persons" and in God's self-giving act of creation. We shall have more opportunity to consider the importance of those effects. But first we should attempt to understand the mysticism of negation and ascent.

No writings provide a more impressive instance of this name-less mysticism than the sermons of the 14th century German Dominican Meister Eckhart. A formidable theologian as well as a daring mystic, Eckhart does not allow his eagle's flight to eclipse the specific demands of Christian tradition. Indeed, he couches his mystical theory in the classical concepts of scholastic theology. Thus he repeats St. Thomas' principle that God is Being. With his great Dominican predecessor, Eckhart refers to *Exodus* 3, 19 where God, instead of revealing His name, declares that He is the one who is. Since names merely define the limits of Being, no other names than the one of pure Being apply to God. For Eckhart it also follows that, if God is Being, creatures as creatures are not. This may seem to desacralize creation. But the divine Being is not separated from the creature: it constitutes the very core of its reality. The creature's true Being *is* God, even though *as creature* it has nothing in common with God. In man this true Being becomes manifest, but only at the end of the inward journey.

God supremely *is*. Yet if divine Being were not self-expressive, it would neither recognize itself nor communicate itself. What then initiates the "manifestation" of Being? According to Eckhart, self-contained simplicity is the first principle which initiates all inward and outward manifestation of divine Being, as the *One* God is the principle from which all "otherness" proceeds and to which it must return. In His aboriginal unity God reveals His disposition to break out into multiplicity.

When the Silence *actually* manifests itself in the *Word*, it becomes fertile—the Father. In the sound of the Word God receives a name, a specific nature. That nature consists in relatedness, a multiplicity occurring within the divine unity. The Father is the generating principle of God's manifestation *within* Himself. But God also manifests **Himself** *outwardly* in His creation. Though the creature's core is God's one Being, its createdness distinguishes it from that Being. According to their Being all creatures from all eternity dwell in God's Word, while according to their separate existence in time they develop in an order of succession and exclusion.

To modern Christians the union between the Eternal Word and the realm of creation may appear to imply a dangerous confusion of the natural order with the "supernatural" one in which the relations between the divine persons take place. But our own separation between God's eternal and His temporal manifestation merely reveals a world view in which the finite reality has lost its religious symbolism. To the early Greek Fathers each finite creature reflects God's eternal Image. Few among our contemporaries know how to read a poem as partaking in the divine self-expression of the Eternal Word. Yet our oldest spiritual tradition assimilates the ultimate meaning of all words to God's eternal manifestation in the Logos. Without their divine image words lose their ultimate reference. They flatten into functional units of a closed system, self-referential elements in a no-win game. Early Christians read the cosmos as a Bible of symbols. For us who no longer do this, the world has ceased to speak of God. It lies inert, a body of dead and living matter to be exploited for various purposes. In viewing all creatures within God's eternal manifestation, Eckhart articulated an earlier, more respectful attitude toward creation. In the Son all creatures possess their own achetypal image. The Eternal Word contains the entire outward explosion of the world in time. In their archetypal image they remain within the Trinity; in their temporal appearance they move outside the circle of God's unity. The following text describes the eternal birth of the Son, and through His birth, that of the entire creation. The Eternal Word contains the whole outward explosion of creation in time. That creation possesses its archetypal image in the Son. But while the Son remains within the Trinity, the creatures in time move outside the circle of God's unity.

> In this Word, God expresses himself together with all the divine Being, all that God is, as only he can know it. And he knows it as it is, because he is perfect in knowledge and power. Therefore, he is also perfect in self-expression. When he utters his Word, he expresses himself and everything else in a second Person, to whom he gives his own nature. He speaks, and all intelligent spirits re-echoing the Word, repeat his idea, just as rays shining from the sun bear the sun in themselves. So each intelligent spirit is a Word in itself; even though it is not like God's Word in all respects, it has received the power to become a likeness of the Word of God, full of grace.[2]

Conscious creatures, aware of the original dwelling in God's immanent Word, long to overcome the distance that separates their created existence from God and to be reunited as much as their finitude allows, with their divine Archetype.

Eckhart's entire mystical doctrine is based upon the essential union of the soul with God. In the uncreated essence of my Being I remain in the Son with the Father. Eckhart daringly expresses this by claiming that there is something in the soul so closely akin to God that it is already one with Him and it need not even be united to Him because it is already divine. If one were wholly this, he would be both uncreated and unlike any other creature.[3] *That* Being of the soul is not its creaturely existence; it is the eternal Being through which it remains in God. "God's Being is my life," says Eckhart. But if this is so, then what is God's must be mine. And what is mine must be God's. God's is-ness is my is-ness. In my primary Being, in my true essence, I am the living idea of God that continues to dwell in God. In this essential Being God expresses himself in his Eternal Word and, in the Word, in every creature.

That true Being of the created spirit may be called eternal as the Word eternally expresses the Father. The solemn liturgy of the Christmas Night reminds the Christian in the words of Psalm 2 of the Father's eternal generation of the Son in an eternal now: "You are my Son. I have begotten You today." *Filius meus es tu. Ego hodie genui te.* The Father begets the Son *today*, in an eternal *now* (*hodie*) and in that same *now* He begets me in the Son. The now of creation and the now of God's self-expression are identical, because the creature remains *essentially* in the Son, and the Son in the creature. Like all creatures, the soul also dwells outside this essential Being. It alone, however, is called to be converted to that eternal Being by becoming aware of its divine essence. Only when the soul turns fully to its divine essence can it truly claim to be reborn as the Son of God, in the Eternal Word. "The Father ceaselessly begets his Son and what is more, he begets me as his Son—the self-same Son! Indeed, He begets me not only as his Son but as himself and himself as myself, begetting me in his own nature, his own being."[4] For Eckhart this means that the spiritual person converts himself to that pure Being for which even the word "God" is inadequate. "For before there were creatures, God was not god, but rather he was what he was."[5] In order to be able to refer to it Eckhart calls that nameless Being beyond manifestation the *Godhead*. In the Godhead there is only unity and silence. "God acts; the Godhead does not. It has nothing to do and there is nothing going on in it."[6] It is the ultimate silence at the end of the return.

·4·

The Poverty of God

What I find at the deepest level of myself is nameless, so nameless, says Eckhart, that God Himself in entering that depth loses His own name. "Back in the Womb from which I came I had no god and merely *was*, myself."[1] "Womb" is capitalized here and "god" is not capitalized. The Godhead *is* before it is named: Being as such has no names. Even the creature in its essence must remain nameless in the pure core of its divine Being. Here I do not will or desire anything beyond what I am. I am what I want and I want what I am. In my uncreated Being I rest, untrammeled even by God. In its ultimate identity Being is what it is or, as Adonai said to Moses, the One Who is. Only in my creaturely existence does "God" confront me. "God" is the name that man invents after a long religious history. First he conceives of the gods, then of *God*. But that pure Being, Eckhart's God- head, remains beyond what we so confidently name "God." "God" belongs to the order of manifestation. And so do all his revealed names, even the most sacred, revealed names of the Divine Persons. For Eckhart the Godhead precedes the divine hypostases of the

39

Father, the Son, and the Holy Ghost. Being surpasses all divine names.

To reach that primeval poverty, my poverty, which for Eckhart is also God's poverty, is the goal of the mystical journey. To attain it, the soul must abandon not only its possessions and its self-will, but also its creature-ly identity and even its "God." In his most radical sermon, "Blessed Are the Poor," Eckhart admonishes, "If one wants to be truly poor, he must be as free from his creature will as when he had not been born." We must become totally detached from that individual existence to which we are so attached. We *know* that this little self is insignificant, but we think we had better hold on to it anyway, since without it, we may have nothing left. That is precisely the self we should surrender, according to Eckhart, if we are to partake of the wealth of God's own poverty.

Inevitably we will become discouraged about our efforts to comply with the requirement of absolute poverty. More seriously, we may feel that we have disappointed God. But for Eckhart the soul that still worries about the quality of its relationship with God has not become truly poor. Indeed, it must give up all ambition to acquire any knowledge of God. "He shall be quit and empty of all knowledge, so that no knowledge of God exists in him." As long as we are still concerned about finding a place for God in ourselves, we are not truly poor. God must create His *own* place in me. Indeed, Eckhart insists, eventually we must free ourselves of the "God" we know, for that is still a private possession. "We pray that we may be rid of God, and taking the truth, break into eternity, where the highest angels and souls too, are like what I was in my *primal* existence when I wanted what I was, and when I was what I wanted."[2]

That ultimate poverty is also the true humility. Too often we confuse humility with false modesty. We secretly hope that if we accuse ourselves of imperfection, God may contradict us, assuring us that we are not all that bad. But God will not contradict us, for the imperfection is real and goes to the core of our existence. That existence itself needs conversion. True humility consists in the *honest* acceptance of my imperfection. The meaning of this humility and this poverty is not simply that of being a means to an end. It is not motivated, as many think, by the idea that by giving up ambition and possession now I shall be compensated for it later. Rather than being a means, poverty is a method of giving way to God. Since to be united with God *is* simply to be devoid of oneself, poverty and humility are the goal! For Eckhart *God means absolute emptiness and poverty.*

This invites us to reflect for a moment on the meaning of the monastic lifestyle. Many outsiders look with envy at a life of contemplation, but they feel no reward, however desirable, could compensate for the hard and continuous sacrifices it requires. This clearly is not at all how most monks feel about their life. By and large they do not experience their existence, however austere, as a *sacrifice*. Some may feel a special vocation to suffer and do penance for others. But vicarious sacrifice certainly does not define the full meaning of monasticism. The example of monastic silence clearly illustrates this. For a person living in constant distraction, silence demands indeed a considerable sacrifice of his natural inclinations. But in the monastic vocation, silence is anything but the deliberate immolation of a positive value. It rather intends to return to the word its original impact. In my conversations with monks I have frequently noticed a certain diffidence toward speech, as if truly important matters could not be entrusted to it. Yet their words, often clumsily articulated, appear to contain a density of meaning that only silence and reflectiveness convey. Silence intensifies rather than attenuates communication. Not wanting to abuse words, the silent monk avoids chitchat and thereby enhances the value of speech. He does not "deprive" himself of speech in anticipation of a future reward. Nor does he "sacrifice" material possessions, personal ambitions or professional prestige. In all these forms of spiritual abstinence the relative value vanishes before the absolute one. To choose one *is* to eliminate the other. Poverty *itself* enriches: the uncluttered life yields its own reward.

To me the most striking quality of the monastic life is not denial, nor even the pursuit of personal perfection, but humility. In his deeply spiritual *Christ, the Ideal of the Monk*, Dom Columbia Marmion, O.S.B. describes the monastic ideal as one of a total openness to life uninhibited by private desires and ambitions. The monk places little stake in personal needs or achievements. He acquits himself of his task as well as he can without feeling the need to justify his existence by his work. Whether it ideally suits his talents, or even whether it fulfils his emotional needs, he considers secondary to the fact that it has been assigned to him. What *he* does matters little as long as it is done. Outsiders often find such a concept of work shockingly impersonal. Why should a man who has earned a doctorate be requested to spend his time scrubbing milk cans? But unselfish devotion to an objective task rewards more than the ever receding promises of a career dedicated to personal advancement.

How well he qualifies for his work, how much it will be appreciated by others, or even how many will profit by it makes little difference to the monk. He rather concentrates on developing that humanly and divinely most desirable attitude of humor which takes seriously only what deserves utmost seriousness—God alone. Most of us, especially most of us academics, tend to take ourselves and our work terribly seriously. But our self-importance appears somewhat pompous to anyone outside our own small circle, profession or specialization. The monk avoids looking ridiculous by refusing to take himself or his work more seriously than they deserve. Measuring them against the backdrop of eternity he rightly judges human concerns to be less than all-significant. Would our human pride not rest on a more solid foundation if we would stop reducing it to the scale of our profession, trade or personal qualities?

The monk spends the better part of his time on what others consider a wasteful activity: singing in an untalented choir. How can anyone concerned with the present course of the world sing all day long? Yet the monk sings through all world-shaking crises, as unconcerned about his musical talents as about the pressure of the times. He sings simply because it is morning, or noon, or night. At the end of the day he sings his thanks for whatever the day has brought. How he "feels" has no effect upon his thanks: every day is a God-given day and, as such, good. This trusting, self-forgetting humility is, I think, a primary condition for any genuinely spiritual life. It certainly is the necessary basis of that spiritual poverty on which, according to Eckhart, the mystical life is built. In poverty and humility I abandon all that I have and even let go of what I am, in order to reach the uncreated core of my being—God's own creating act. God himself dwells in the absolute poverty that knows no possession, not even that of a name. As we move more deeply into that divine poverty, we shall be less and less inclined to place labels on God or His creatures, to pre-establish rigorous standards they must meet, or to raise specific expectations. The readiness to abandon all this conditions that process of "de-creation" (Eckhart's word) in which the soul finds rest in its labors, permanence in its temporality. Through total poverty alone the soul can prepare itself to enter the barren desert of the Godhead.

Eckhart also uses the word *Gelassenheit*. *Gelassenheit* means more than the English resignation. It means waiting in expectation, openness without demands, willingness to be drawn into God's own vacuum. Only through *Gelassenheit* do we reach the point of *nowhere* in the midst of all movement, the nothingness at the heart of all being. We cannot even *actively* seek it. For if we *know* what we are seeking, we shall never find it. As Thomas Merton wrote: "Don't try too hard. Don't be too much concerned about your own perfection and progress from day to day. Once you become aware of yourself as seeker, you become a possessor. You're lost. But if you are content to be lost, you will be found without knowing it, precisely because you are lost. For you are at the last nowhere, which is where God is." Negative theology means far more than that we find no adequate names for God. It means, on a practical-spiritual level, that there exists no failproof method for reaching

God, and hence that my only hope lies in the humble awareness of my inadequacy. My lack of faith, my psychic limitations (including the ones that spiritually incapacitate), the radical worldliness of my age, this is the dark cloud I must enter deliberately if I am to find God at all. It is the cloud of my own estrangement, my own waylessness. No spiritual life can take off without passing through an intense awareness of the emptiness of the creature. This is the lasting message of all negative theology, especially of Meister Eckhart's lesson of absolute poverty.

The message seems far removed from the aspirations of a culture predominantly bent on self-fulfillment and self-achievement. Yet that is perhaps the very reason why it so powerfully appeals to those who seek to lead a spiritual life in our time. The practical a-theism which surrounds us excludes any ready access to the divine realm. Current secularism has questioned far more than the doctrine of God. It has jeopardized the possibility of lifting our minds and hearts beyond the objective world we know and control. The very attitude toward existence required for the idea of God to make sense has vanished. We have become the efficient, objective and responsible inhabitants of a well-organized closed world. Amazingly enough, deep down men and women still nurture the aspiration of breaking through the enclosure into the free space of transcendence. To realize this aspiration, however, they must first become aware of their own moral and spiritual predicament. A precondition for spiritual life is the willingness to enter into our own radical profaneness, to recognize the practical atheism by which we conduct our affairs and to admit that it is not only the name of God we have forgotten but also the natural piety which alone enables man to speak that name truthfully. The aspirant to spiritual life must learn a new attitude before he learns new concepts or practices. Unconditional trust without knowing what it is we trust, willingness to let go without knowing whether anyone will ever catch us, preparedness to wait without knowing whether we will be met. Total looseness and unconditional trust are the virtues negative theology teaches us to cultivate. There could be no more appropriate lesson in our time.

·5·

The Second Negation

Negative theology has not spoken the final word about spiritual life. Having led the soul into the darkness of unknowing and undoing, it stops there, as if God Himself were mere darkness. Yet the cloud in which God dwells is not that of His, but of my, darkness. God, as Eckhart himself teaches, is light unto Himself. He reveals Himself in the brightness of His Eternal Word. The Godhead is not a barren desert, but a fertile process of self-communication. As Ruusbroec writes: "In this darkness there shines and is born an incomprehensible light which is the Son of God in whom we behold eternal light. And in this light one becomes seeing."[1] The divine "emptiness" constantly generates itself and, in itself, its other, the creature. The divine silence speaks its one and only Word, and, in that Word, all words, symbols and manifestations. The soul also, once it has reached the divine emptiness, must follow the divine expression in the Word and, *within* that Word, in all creation. The person whom Ruusbroec describes as seeing the light in divine darkness and then becoming that light himself is the one who has become totally poor and genuinely humble. Once he or she has

47

ascended the ladder of negation and moved into the wilderness "that wastes us" (Merton), there remains a final step to be taken. The genuinely poor person must kick down the ladder itself. He or she must not persist in negation, for denial itself is only a creaturely attempt to reach beyond creation. God himself is not negative: He has spoken and manifested Himself. Hence the language of negation cannot have the last word. If we ever reach the divine unity, we must move where God Himself moves, that is, from the principle of generation into the principle of manifestation and, completing the sacred circle, back to its origin in the principle of unity. Upon the denial of the creature follows a more radical denial in which the spiritual person denies the negation itself. Some mystics have remained in the movement of denial. To them God is neither darkness nor light, neither nonbeing nor being. Buddhists who refuse to name the Absolute are not "atheists" like the secular men and women of our own culture: they are mystics of silence. Christianity, the religion of the Word, has never been satisfied with ultimate silence. Some of its mystics have occasionally come close to it, as when Eckhart claimed that in the Godhead there is neither Father, Son, nor Holy Spirit. All spiritual life begins by renouncing creaturely attachments and even creaturely concepts of God. But it proceeds by the awareness that the negative perspective is itself a created one. At that point a religion of manifestation invites the spiritual pilgrim to sacrifice his own perspective and to follow the Absolute in its manifestation. In this second, more fundamental negation he first fully acknowledges his own efforts, even his ascent to the Absolute, as being intrinsically inadequate. No spiritual effort brings me to my goal without my being brought there in grace.

In sublime words the blessed Jan Ruusbroec describes the participation in God's inner life to which the soul courageous enough to *abandon* itself to divine love is invited.

> [In that darkness] the spirit is embraced by the Holy Trinity and dwells forever within the superessential Unity, in rest and fruition. And in that same Unity, according to its fruitfulness, the Father dwells in the Son and the Son in the Father, and all creatures dwell in Both. And this is above the distinction of the Persons. . . . Here, there arise and begin an eternal going out and an eternal work which is without beginning; for here there is a beginning with beginning. For after the Almighty Father had perfectly comprehended Himself in the ground of His fruitfulness, so the Son, the Eternal Word of the Father, came forth as the Second Person in the Godhead. And, through the Eternal Birth, all creatures have come forth in eternity, before they were created in time.[2]

That Trinitarian life to which the spiritual person is called is life in unity. But that unity itself is fertile. It generates; it communicates itself. In the self-generated communication the darkness turns into light, a light in which the spiritual person "becomes seeing" and which he or she brings out into the world. Beyond the dark night of Eckhart's mysticism dwells the God of whom the hymn of Matins sings:

> *O God who dwells beyond the night*
> *As in a garment wrapped in light;*
> *You kindle faith within man's heart,*
> *Preserving him from endless dark.*[3]

The soul united to God as self-manifest also embraces all creatures in which He outwardly manifests Himself. Partaking of the love between Father and Son, it likewise participates in God's creative love of all creatures. In a world of multiplicity it recognizes the God it has found in a multitude of His self-manifesting relationships. Those relationships between God and the creatures in which he manifests Himself the spiritual Christian calls *love*.

·6·

The Divine Love
of the Creature

In its spiritual love for the creatures the soul participates in God's own relationship to them. But does the term "love" appropriately express the relationship from the creature to God? Does it not introduce a presumptuous familiarity in the relationship between God and man? Granting that there is an Agape descending from God to the creature, could man, even the most spiritual man or woman, ever assume that divine flow in his or her own being and return it to its origin? Christian mystics have never doubted that they can, and they have made this participation in God's own love the basis of their attitude toward their fellow creatures. Yet their confidence rests on the searing purgation of desire which they had to undergo before attaining the divine love of the finite. For in order to be able to love a creature with God's love, the lover must first forsake his own, private, possessive love of the creature. To love the creature as God loves it, is to love it *for its own sake*, not for my sake.

While our ordinary attitude tends to possess, manipulate, and control the other, divine charity allows the creature to be what it is. God grants the creature an independence that allows it even to turn against its Creator. He takes the risk taken by all wholly unselfish love, that the other will not return one's love, that he or she will crush the lover. In *The Ascent of Mount Carmel* (I, 13) John of the Cross describes the painful process of conversion required by such a pure love:

> In order to arrive at possessing everything, desire to possess nothing.
> In order to arrive at being everything, desire to be nothing.
> In order to arrive at knowing everything, desire to know nothing.[1]

Many have criticized this radical "renunciation" as being inhuman while rejecting the idea of man's participation in the divine love for the creature as presumptuous. Indeed, taken separately, the idea of renouncing the creation is no more Christian than that of claiming to possess a divine love for it. But in spiritual life one implies the other. The Christian mystic does not forsake the creature. He or she merely attempts to subdue the natural possessiveness which constantly drives us to exploit the other for selfish goals, in order to enable us to perceive the other as God perceives him or her.

Unselfishness is, of course, extraordinarily difficult in human relationship and no saint, to my knowledge, has ever claimed to have achieved it completely. Lest we take a firm hold of the other, we fear, his or her "otherness" may submerge our own identity. Hence we seldom leave the other person free to be what he is, and we force him within the restrictive pattern of our own needs. How seldom has our love liberated the other! How often has our selfish attachment enslaved him or her! Instead of enriching others we mostly draw them into the narrow circle of our own restricted lives. We further bind those who were only half free themselves. Merely human love inevitably turns possessive and exclusive.

But if human love is by nature possessive, can we ever hope to love unselfishly while loving humanly? The question is legitimate enough, but it dispenses the spiritual aspirant neither from loving nor from attempting to love unselfishly. In *The Works of Love* Kierkegaard presents some sober advice to those who strive to fulfil the commandment, *Love thy neighbor*. To love the other as one's neighbor, he informs us, means to love the person whom God has placed on my path, primarily *because God has placed* that person there. Hence a husband must love his wife first and foremost because he is bound to her by divine ties, not because she is the woman he has chosen for himself or because she pleases him more than others. This seemingly ordinary rule of Christian conduct provides the key for understanding what is perhaps the most distinctive and certainly the most admirable quality of Christian mysticism, namely, its capacity to embrace all creatures in the one act of divine love. The Christian mystic loves all life, also deformed, sickly or even dying life, because he or she cherishes that life *for its own sake*, not for its capacity to please or fulfil him or her. He learns to perceive God as present in the creature—not merely in that divine core where God's creative act touches the creature, but also in its finite individuality, its ungodly imperfection and its fragile vulnerability. The Christian mystic understands that also in its finitude the creature possesses a divine meaning. In his creative act God manifests not merely his identity, but also his difference. Not only the divine spark, of which Eckhart wrote, shines divinely, but also the often coarse and always finite, created individuality which hides this spark. When God creates in time He acts differently than when He begets His eternal Word: here He manifests Himself in identity, there in difference. Yet the difference forms an essential part of the divine manifestation. That is what the Christian mystic understands when he attempts to love the creature for its own sake. Angelus Silesius shocked his readers when he wrote that without the creature God would not be God. Yet in this statement we hear the authentic voice of Christian mysticism. For without the creature God is He who is. Only for his creatures does He adopt the name of God. Each creature forms a humble, totally dependent, but nevertheless unique part of God's manifestation. The God-seeking soul must enter into this manifestation beyond the dark that lies behind all manifestation. Those who halt at the divine darkness never enter the divine life as it *actively develops*. For that life also descends into the creatures. In the mystery of the Incarnation God has supremely revealed how divinely the creature matters to Him. No mysticism can claim to be Christian that does not include a spiritual love for the creature. Teresa of Avila accused herself of having neglected the *humanity* of Christ in the early stages of her spiritual development. In doing so, she rightly felt, she had deprived herself of a central aspect of God's self-manifestation.

Its presence to all creation has made Christian mysticism such a vital power in Western culture. By and large Christian spirituality has been marvelously earthly and humane. We might almost regard it as a divine humanism. Who in thirteenth century Italy had a deeper impact upon his culture than Francis of Assisi, an uneducated man, of average intelligence, but a visionary who saw all creation filled with divine life? After him we looked with different eyes at nature, animals, people. We wrote different poetry and we fashioned different paintings. We lived and loved differently. Ignatius of Loyola, a soldier, sparse in words and of limited emotions with little aesthetic sense and no poetic talent, another man altogether, nevertheless had one thing in common with Francis: he loved God excessively and he knew Him present in His creatures. He also, this barely cultured saint, exercised an unparallelled influence on the culture of his age. Teresa of Avila, a cloistered nun of little formal educaton, ambitious only in the quest of humility and abnegation, created an unprecedented ideal of confident, assertive womanhood and changed the Spanish civilization. Catherine of Siena, who could not even claim the rank of full membership in a religious order, at a time when no women other than queens and princesses enjoyed any public status, managed to persuade the Pope to abandon his exile in Avignon and to return to Rome. Christian contemplatives have always felt the need to follow God in His "work" in creation. In the concluding "Contemplation to Obtain Divine Love" of his *Spiritual Exercises*, Ignatius of Loyola invites us to meditate upon the presence of God in His creatures, not as a passive presence but as an energetic one that actively operates in all things.

As we saw, to pursue *God* in the creatures rather than the satisfaction of one's desires does not come naturally. It is no coincidence that most known Christian mystics have been canonized saints, that is, men and women of heroic virtue. To love creatures requires no effort, particularly if they are lovable—we all do that as a matter of course. Even to renounce part of creation is not too difficult for a spiritual person. But to love creation, to be deeply involved with it, and yet to remain detached from it, demands more than common virtue. We know John of the Cross' advice. Saint Ignatius formulates a similar rule in his third degree of humility.

The first degree of humility, he writes, demands that we be ready to forsake the whole world, even life itself, rather than to offend God's Majesty. The second degree consists in showing no preference for either ease or hardship, joy or suffering, provided that there be the same opportunity to serve God. It accepts all experiences of life with equal gratitude from God's hands. Some pages in the so-called Quietist literature have praised with lyrical eloquence this attitude which culminates in spiritual life. And yet Ignatius adds a third degree. To be perfect the Christian should *prefer* suffering, poverty and humiliation to ease, riches, and honor. Even if moral perfection should be equal, he should deliberately choose what is more difficult and more painful. Only after having acquired such a disposition will the spiritual person be fully able to perceive and to love God in all things. Only he who goes beyond mere indifference and resignation will be safe from the illusions of selfishness in his relationships with the world. It would be easy to reject the pursuit of such an attitude as a masochistic exercise. But in presenting this position, quite common in Christian spirituality, Ignatius by no means claims that suffering is in itself preferable to comfort. He simply shows a realistic knowledge of human nature in assuming that, left to its natural inclinations, it will move in a direction opposite to indifference.

As we observed earlier, spiritual poverty understood as that total openness which favors no personal preferences is far more than a means to a spiritual end. It itself is the end, the ideal. But this end cannot be attained by the mere resolution to be indifferent. It requires going against the grain of inclinations that naturally move into the opposite direction. Mortification is the price the mystic must pay for returning safely to a full involvement with the created world. The price is not only high. It is hazardous as well. For a positive welcoming of suffering and pain may easily degenerate into a sickly dolorism. Spiritual masters, however, advocate the choice of suffering not for its own sake, but *for the love of the suffering Christ*. Saint Ignatius articulates his third degree of humility in the following terms: "If we suppose the first and the second kind attained, that is, if we have already attained some measure of indifference, then whenever the praise and glory of the Divine Majesty would be equally served, in order to imitate and be in reality more like Christ Our Lord, I desire and choose poverty with Christ poor, rather than riches; insults with Christ loaded with them, rather than honors; I desire to be accounted as worthless and a fool for Christ, rather than to be esteemed as wise and prudent in this world. So Christ was treated before me."[2] Christ is the only mediator, in the practico-spiritual order as well as in the theological one. In returning the divine love to the created world Christians need the divinely revealed model of virtue and abnegation as much as they need the revelation of the Word in Christ in order to attain the Father. The suffering humanity of Christ has been the constant exemplar and the almost exclusive motivation in the practice and theory of Christian asceticism. The purgation and illumination of the soul have always followed the pattern of an *imitation of Christ*.

·7·

The Imitation of Christ

The preceding invites us to reflect a little more on the role of Christ in Christian mysticism. What does Christ mean to the Christian mystic? One answer, often given or assumed, we may outright reject: Christ belongs to that general patrimony of his religious tradition from which the Christian mystic draws his symbols, and occasionally his inspiration, but which has no direct impact upon his essentially private, nontraditional process of interiorization. No attentive reader of Christian texts could possibly accept such an interpretation. Its popular success is probably due to the equally common, even more erroneous thesis that all types of mysticism are fundamentally alike; the different expressions it takes articulate a common experience. We shall waste no time on an opinion which has been refuted by all available evidence. Yet we must admit that the role of Christ, though substantial in all Christian mystics, varies from one to another. In Eckhart, for instance, Christ is the model that instructs. But His humanity appears to play no primary role in the mystical interiorization. For others, such as Saint Teresa, Christ serves as model precisely by being the main focus of mystical love. Only if I love Christ shall I desire to be conformed to Him. His example becomes effective only insofar as He fascinates me as the beloved fascinates the lover.

But why should the Christian mystic "love" Christ? Buddhism does not request its followers to "love" the Siddhartha. It even would frown upon such an attachment to a person. To the Christian Christ presents the perfect creature, the only one she or he may hope to love as God loves the creature. Since Christ's humanity is filled with His divinity, it is the one creature that we can, under any circumstances, love without having to fear the selfish interference of a deceptive nature. The love for Christ allows no room for illusion. That love may be sensuous or even erotic (as it has been for some mystics); it nevertheless remains directed at the one divine Person. In this hypostatic union of a divine and a human nature Christ is the religious archetype of all creatures. He presents, in an ideal mode, the creature filled with God, and, therefore, lovable in God. In loving him who is full of God, the spiritual person learns how to love all creatures, since all, in some degree, contain a spark of that of divine life, the fullness of which resides in Christ.

As a soldier in the Belgian army I once worked in a military hospital. My ward of heart and kidney patients was supervised by an elderly nun, a gracious woman of refined manners. I clearly remember the sight of this frail, aristocratic lady tending her unruly Flemish flock. Yet for all their incongruity they got along splendidly. For her each of these hard-drinking, loud-cursing soldiers *was* Christ. Intrigued, I wondered what she could possibly have *meant* by that. I could see how a spiritual person equipped with a goodly amount of virtue and a developed sense of humor could have wanted to love them *as if* they were Christ. But for her there was no "as if." The matter was straight and simple. She saw in them the same divine life which attains its fullness in Christ. The ordinary person, when told to love Christ in each creature, looks for similarity, for a common pattern of behavior. And, of course, he or she soon becomes disappointed. For few people look or behave like Christ. But such is not the spiritual person's perspective. For him or her, others represent Christ in a much deeper sense, because the same divine life moves in them, of which He possesses the fullness. Only spiritual writers have developed this idea, but it is the true, Christian view of creation.

It is not surprising, then, that the great lovers of Christ, even those who secluded themselves from others, have also been the great lovers of humanity. Saint Francis of Assisi, that ardent lover of the human Christ, revolutionized love itself in the West. Christianity, whatever we may think of its historical record, has taught people to love. It has provided a model, divinely lovable, in whom to love all creatures. The humanity of Christ, then, may not be the *ultimate* object of mystical love, but for most Christian mystics that humanity nevertheless mediates their inclusion of all creatures in God. In order to appreciate fully this Christocentric character of our mysticism, we must realize that in Christianity the love for the creature in God is not an optional, secondary matter. Ours is, through and through, an incarnational religion. The central mystery of the Incarnation tolerates no separation of the love of God from the love of the creature. In pursuing a contemplative life it may seem more convenient to withdraw from the created world altogether, to enter into oneself and to seek God by removing oneself, as much as possible, from His creation. But this is not the Christian way, and Christian mystics again and again have denounced it, from Ruusbroec's polemics with the *Begharden* to the eighteenth-century Quietist condemnations. For Christian mysticism a loving involvement with the created world is essential, not accidental.

Yet, one might insist, why should my love for Christ's humanity require that I imitate Him in His suffering? Why concentrate on the most humiliating aspect of His Incarnation? Was it not enough that He had to undergo this? What can we contribute by following Him in His agony? The answer, I believe, lies in the inevitable union of love and suffering. Only in suffering does love prove its authenticity. Lovers of all ages have sought out hardship and denial, not merely as a token of love to the beloved, but to authenticate it for themselves. Suffering alone, if freely accepted, safeguards love against selfishness. For the creature at least, even for that creature who was personally united to God, loving means more than giving oneself—it means giving oneself *up* for the other.

Suffering is by its very nature passive. In it I cease to be the center of decision and I submit to a higher power. My natural inclination goes in the opposite direction. I always like to be in control of the situation, to direct it from my own inner center. Even in loving a fellow creature, or God Himself, I like to show my devotion to the other by *doing* something for him or her. But the problem with *doing* is that, in the end, I always do as I please. Like it or not, in doing I remain self-centered, and no self-centered love can be divine love. Hence the mystic has no choice but, at a certain point, to stop doing and take the road of suffering.

Suffering alone removes the center from myself and allows the other to feel that he or she is not being manipulated. Our impact upon others is often greater during those periods when circumstances painfully confront us with our own, very deep limitations. Frequently it is only in those periods that we truly start *giving*, because we were forced to stop manipulating. We can love creatures unselfishly only—and hence divinely—after our self-love has been crushed. Paradoxically, the broken self appears to be the only self worth giving.

Christian piety has always sought an intimate presence to Jesus' Passion rather than a mere commemoration of the past. It seeks "compassion" in the present with what Jesus felt *then*. To be with Him in the *present* of His agony and rejection when no triumph was in sight, that is to be where He really was. But to be present to His hour means more than to be present there in feeling. It means entering into the dark reality of my own suffering, loneliness and failure. Only in the brokenness and pain of life am I with Him where He continues to live His agony. Unfortunately, when thinking of Jesus' Passion we only recall His divine will, His human innocence and, above all, His unique mission. Even to the suffering of the saints we attribute a meaning and dignity which are lacking in our own suffering consciousness. Following a clearly perceived vocation they entered willingly into what we assume they knew to be a night of purification. How different from my own suffering! Does it ever go beyond the pain of thin-skinned selfishness, the disappointment of vulgar ambitions, the frustration of unpurified desires, and the loneliness of self-inflicted isolation? How dare I call what possesses so little dignity "suffering"? Whenever I lift my eyes to the crucified Savior it is mostly to move away from my private misery, certainly not to move *into* it.

Nevertheless, Christian piety teaches that very suffering of mine, however despicable and even sinful in its origins, *is* Jesus' agony in me. Comparing my pain with Jesus' Passion may seem blasphemous. But all suffering began with a curse. His as well as mine. Whether pain has its roots in private weakness and failure, or whether it is inflicted by an entire universe of weakness and failure, the effect remains the same. To him who suffers, suffering means always failure. Jesus' words on the cross—My God, my God, why have you forsaken me? —do not express the attitude of one who is performing a clearly understood, effective sacrifice. They say what suffering has said from the beginning of the world and what it still says in me: In this I am hopelessly alone.

A great deal has been written about the purifying, strengthening qualities of suffering. These qualities may be known to him who has suffered, but not to him who suffers. Within my actual suffering I detect no meaning. It would cease to exist or, at least, lose much of its sting, if I could only experience a universal meaning in it. To suffer is to be alone. No one can follow the sufferer into this most private world. Physicians and psychologists attempting to alleviate human pain classify it in categories. But none of their general terms—depression, feeling of loss, etc.—describes the intensely private experience of pain. It is like nothing else and, in it, I am like no one else. Indeed, it is the only part of myself that is exclusively me, that bears my name. No one enters this most intimate solitude of my own pain.

Whatever the undignified causes of my suffering—
and they are all undignified in a cursed world, for Jesus
as well as for me—my suffering is my very existence—
dignified or not! It is isolation with no past to comfort
and no future to hope for, the empty desert of a bleak
present. Frequently the desert of the soul is one from
which God also has withdrawn. Its emptiness signals
rejection. Does God ever answer the cry: Why have you
forsaken me? Most times we suppress the question as
impious. I know I cannot expect a divine interference
for every pain that strikes me. After all, this world follows a course of its own and a cause—self-inflicted or
other-inflicted—must have its effect. But deep down I
cannot help feeling lost in a machinery the designer of
which chose to ignore my anticipated distress. Thus Jesus also felt lost when petty fanaticism and gratuitous
resentment, rather than a grand, predetermined
scheme of salvation brought Him to the cross.

"Were you *there* when they nailed Him to the tree?"
Was I *there* in my suffering? For that is where He is being crucified—in me, not in Jerusalem. There stands
the tree from which grace flows. Grace is not a pipeline
from which each taps according to his needs: it is my individual election, as personal as my suffering. Indeed, it
is that suffering. In this world there can be no grace but
through redemptive suffering. To encounter God's ago-
nizing grace I must walk into the bleak desert of my private pain and humiliation. Perhaps I shall be able to ac-
complish no more than silently to accept my inability to
accept. But not more is expected: to confront my bitter-
ness, rebellion, greed, jealousy, rage, impatience is to
encounter Jesus' agony in my own. I must find Jesus'
agony also in those private worlds of suffering around

me, which I am so reluctant to explore and so unable to comprehend. Here also I am invited to accept, without understanding, Jesus' agony in the uncouth, the uncivilized, the unlovable. On Good Friday failure itself has become redemptive. That Jesus fails in me is the joyous mystery of the union between God and me.

·8·

The Way of Purgation

Our reflection on suffering has led us naturally into what Christian tradition considers to be the beginning of all spiritual life, the purgation of the soul. In
this first stage of contemplation the soul actively attempts to loosen its attachments through exercises of abnegation and mortification and, if mystical states follow, becomes passively purified in senses and mind.
Thus in discussing the traditional division of the stages
of purgation, illumination and union, we must avoid
conceiving of spiritual life as if it were divided into
three separate phases that follow one another in recti-
linear succession.

The passive purgation, according to John of the
Cross, does not occur until the soul has already become
considerably "illuminated" through meditation and
even, if we may believe other mystics, through quiet
contemplation. Higher illumination necessitates a
higher form of purgation. John of the Cross applies the
metaphor of the night to both passive purgation and illumination, because one is intrinsically connected with
the other.

Even the distinction between the active and the passive phases of spiritual life must not be pressed too far. The author of *The Cloud of Unknowing*, an anonymous English text of the fourteenth century, suggests that the higher part of the "active life" already coincides with the lower part of the passive contemplation where the soul is introduced to meditation, a sorrowful awareness of the soul's wretched state, a compassion with Christ's suffering, and a feeling of gratitude for God's wonderful gifts. A person cannot actively pursue religious perfection unless he or she is to some extent a contemplative. Nor can he or she become fully contemplative without actively translating what he or she contemplates into virtue and good deeds. The higher part of contemplation is wholly caught up in a dark "cloud of unknowing" in which the soul confronts the naked Being of God Himself, and Him only. After we have moved into that darkness, it all depends on God how far He takes us into His own inner life. "But in the higher part of the contemplative life a man is definitely reaching above himself, and is inferior to none but God."

One more preliminary remark. A successful entering of the purgative way presupposes that the soul has already become *awake* to the love of God. It is not sufficient for the novice to be full of spiritual desire. He or she must be "awakened" to it in a manner over which he or she has no control. Many saints, as we know, have undergone rather abrupt conversions to spiritual life. It is generally assumed that mystics also experience a clear "awakening" to a higher state of spiritual awareness. Yet in *The Psychology of the Mystics*, the eminent philosopher Joseph Maréchal claims that for most people that awakening occurs gradually in the course of ordinary prayer. It concludes a process that has started with meditation, has then moved into a more inward recollection which, in due time, has turned into a state of habitual dwelling in the presence of God. In any case, whether the soul awakens slowly or suddenly, a new awareness of God's presence conditions any significant progress in the process of purgation. *Love* must come first. The soul must be centered on *God* rather than on itself before the real purgation can start.

Let us now briefly consider the so-called active purgation. At this stage the soul labors at overcoming the major obstacles that obstruct its spiritual progress. In her classic *Mysticism* Evelyn Underhill informs us that the active purgation consists of two forms: *detachment*, intended to sever the existing ties of desire, and *mortification*, the deliberate choice of what is disagreeable, painful or humiliating, intended to reverse habitual patterns of affection and behavior. In the religious vows the church has institutionalized the active pursuit of spiritual detachment. Through poverty, chastity and obedience the candidate for spiritual life places himself on the road to the kind of absolute poverty of which Eckhart speaks in the sermon "Blessed Are the Poor."

Yet clearly, observing the three religious vows does not automatically purify the soul. At most they provide a frame within which the soul may actively pursue its own perfection. Nothing in spiritual life occurs "automatically," even though its major developments happen passively. Small attachments within the protective boundaries of the religious state are as detrimental to spiritual progress as major ones in the secular life. Vows and rules do not dispense a person from a serious, personal application at the task of purifying himself or herself.

In the first book of *The Ascent of Mount Carmel* and the first eight chapters of *The Dark Night of the Soul* John of the Cross describes the active night of the senses, the detachment of any pleasure that follows the fulfilment of sensuous desire. All creatures, he writes, are nothing, and the affections caused by our attachment to them are less than nothing, a mere negative impediment in the attainment of the one true reality. "What has the creature to do with the Creator? What has sensual to do with spiritual? Visible with invisible? Temporal with eternal?"[1] The phrase could have been written by Meister Eckhart, except that for John the creature plays and important role in this preparation of religious life. The images and ideas acquired in meditation help the soul to purify itself.

But, John insists, the soul must purify itself of the *desire* of the creature, more than of the creature itself. Inner detachment matters, not physical privation. John explicitly warns against excessive mortification, which focuses undue attention on bodily desires. Not the pleasure, but the desire of pleasure, its self-contracting aspect by which I turn back into myself, must be renounced. Pleasure is a necessary component of physical life. For one who is hungry, not to enjoy eating is neither natural nor desirable. But to eat merely for the sake of pleasure deflects the soul from its upward movement. Significantly, John of the Cross posits the love of Christ, not the pursuit of personal perfection as the main motive of all mortification. "Every pleasure if it be not purely for the honor and love of God must be renounced and completely rejected for the love of Jesus Christ."[2] The renunciation of desire must, from the beginning, be motivated by what lies beyond man, rather than by an egocentric concern with moral progress. An ascetic pursuit of virtue for its own sake has no part in Christian mysticism. Even the desire of spiritual perfection must be *God-centered* from the start. Too great a *concern* with one's own condition in no way profits spiritual life.

Meanwhile John's advice is straightforward and uncompromising:

> Strive always to prefer not that which is easiest, but that which is most difficult; not that which is most delectable, but that which is most unpleasing; not that which gives most pleasure, but rather that which gives least. . . . Strive thus to desire to enter into complete detachment and emptiness and poverty with respect to everything that is in the world for Christ's sake.[3]

John insists on detachment with respect to thoughts. Even memory, the entrance gate to spiritual life, presents temptations and must be directed.

Yet this active purgation, however demanding, hardly compares to the passive one that follows the beginning of the mystical graces. Saint John of the Cross devotes the first book of *The Dark Night* (with the exception of the first seven chapters) to the passive purgation of the senses, and the second book to that of the spirit. This is how he announces his subject: "The first purgation or night is bitter and terrible to sense. . . . The second bears no comparison with it, for it is horrible and awful to the spirit."[4] According to John and other spiritual masters this passive purgation follows a period of great spiritual alacrity. Then when "the sun of divine favor is shining most brightly,"[5] God turns all the light into darkness. The soul now finds itself at a point where it is unable to advance to full contemplation and unable to withdraw to meditation. It passes through a "winter of the soul," a period of utter aridity which gives it a positive aversion from spiritual matters without allowing it to experience any pleasure in the ordinary comforts of life. In this "purgatory" (Catherine of Genoa) the soul must become detached from its last attachment, the sensible and spiritual experience of the presence of God. It is now forced to abandon the one support that sustained it through all the hardships and privations of the ascent of Mount Carmel. Henceforth the *experience* of God's love must make room for God alone. For that experience is not God and hence erects a screen between the soul and God's naked presence. This condition of Godlessness, distinct from atheism only by its feeling of utter bereavement and lasting faith, may persist for years. It may be accompanied by obsessions of profanity, temptations to despair, feelings of total rejection. The mystic—for this is a characteristically mystical state—finds himself or herself suspended between heaven and earth without gaining access to either one. The worldly life holds no more attraction. Nor is the mystic able to recover even a minimum of the past spiritual fervor. All that once filled the soul with happiness has lost its meaning and taste: God as well as the world. Nor has anything replaced it. Yet deep down the mystic retains the conviction that God is still there. In the life of Saint Catherine of Siena we read that after she had been tormented by hideous visions of sin, she exclaimed, "Where were you, Lord, when I was tormented by this foulness?" The divine voice answered, "I was in your heart. . . ." In her *Dialogue*, Christ justifies this behavior.

> In order to raise the soul from imperfection I withdraw myself from her sentiment, depriving her of

former consolations . . . which I do in order to hu-
miliate her, and cause her to seek Me in truth and
to prove her in the light of faith, so that she comes
to prudence. Then, if she love Me without thought
of self, and with lively faith and with hatred of her
own sensuality, she rejoices in the time of trouble,
deeming herself unworthy of peace and quietness
of mind . . . . Though she perceives that I have
withdrawn Myself, she does not on that account
look back. But she perseveres with humility in her
exercises, remaining barred in the house of self-
knowledge and continuing to dwell therein, awaits
with lively faith, the coming of the Holy Spirit, that
is of Me, who am the Fire of Love.[6]

Though the passive purgation is the "privilege" of the advanced, in some measure each spiritual person must partake in it. The spiritual desolation, the all too familiar
acedia, which regularly empties our existence of its religious meaning, presents a real similarity with the passive
night of the mystic. It also holds unique opportunities for
advancing in spiritual life. Unfortunately we seldom
grasp the opportunity. As we noted earlier, we rarely
value our own suffering. We dare not compare to the
dark night what takes place in such an imperfect subject.
We forget that any suffering, however humble and humiliating, passively purges the accepting soul. That my
suffering differs from the mystic's should not discourage
me from taking it seriously. Suffering is always unique to
the person who suffers and separates him or her from all
others. What mostly distinguishes the mystic from the
ordinary person is his or her willingness to regard it, even
in its most humiliating aspects, as a most individual vocation. The mystic is ready for the passive purgation because he or she has long learned to accept *all* suffering as
a God-given chance to be purified.

·9·

Illumination and Union

What we call the spiritual illumination, Saint John of the Cross classifies under the night of the mind. There is a significant lesson in this. Spiritual light appears as darkness to the ordinary consciousness. The brightest illuminations, Saint John warns us, appear not to be light at all. Dame Julian of Norwich speaks of "our light in our night!" Tauler refers to the darkness created by a divine light "which by its blinding clearness is dark to human and even angels' understanding, just as the resplendent orb of the sun appears dark to the weak eye."

In the rhythm of spiritual life the purgation of senses and mind gives way to the perception of a new transcendent reality. But it remains a cyclical ascent moving up in spirals that pass through the same succession of purification and illumination on ever higher levels. Even an ordinary religious experience entails a new perception of reality. On the mystical level this consists, above all, in a new awareness of divine presence. To the mystic, God is as present as we are to one another. Indeed, the awareness of an almost tangible presence, marks the breakthrough of the mystical grace in the strict sense of the word. This does not necessarily occur in a sudden flash. It may be a gradual process of interiorization—actively pursued—that eventually results in a more or less permanent state of "quiet." Of course, as the eighteenth-century Quietist controversy has shown, "quiet" is an ambiguous term. Being the point at which the transition from meditation to passive prayer occurs, it may be the final outcome of human effort or the initial stage of infused contemplation. Only in the latter sense could we consider it mystical. No spiritual life can exist without those more passive states of consciousness to which Evelyn Underhill refers as "a self-forgetting attentiveness, a profound concentration, a self-merging, which operates a real communion between the seer and the seen."[1] Yet some such contemplative passivity may be acquired by ordinary human effort. The so-called prayer of simple regard, consisting in a non-discursive attention to God's presence, lies within the ordinary development of any spiritual life. The Quietists have been accused of blurring the line that divides the prayer of simple regard from the prayer of infused quiet.[2] But the saints themselves are not always clear on this distinction. Saint Teresa, for instance, hesitates to call the "prayer of recollection" in which the senses gradually lose their hold as the soul enters into itself, "supernatural" (that is, infused).[3] In any event, all masters agree that some spiritual enlightenment precedes mystical states proper. The passive purgation follows and leads, in turn, to the higher forms of illumination (visions and infused contemplation) which we shall discuss.

In his *Psychology of the Mystics* Maréchal considers the intensive experience of a divine presence *the* most characteristic mystical phenomenon. It certainly is the one that most directly responds to our deepest religious aspirations. We all feel tempted to say with the apostle Philip: "Show us the Father and we shall be satisfied." How it would fill our lives thus truly *to see*. Many a man and a woman would gladly give up everything for that experience. Of course, not every experience of the presence of God is the exclusive privilege of the mystic. Indeed, most of us have, intermittently, felt something of this nature. Yet the mystical experience of presence has a distinctive, almost physical quality. The term "physical" may be misleading, since the highest, exclusively mystical visions are not physical at all. Still they convey an even more intensive feeling of presence. To put it simply, the ordinary feeling of God's presence occurs at a lower degree of intensity than the awareness of a physical presence, while the mystical occurs at the same (indeed it frequently has all the characteristics of an awareness of physical presence) or at a higher degree.

Mystical illumination takes place on several levels. It may be a perception, a vision of the senses. Some psychologists call such phenomena "hallucinations." The term need not be derogatory (as it becomes when identified with hysteria) and I have no objections to it, as long as hallucination simply means *physical awareness which is not provoked by an ordinary sense stimulus.* Thus we may call the apparitions of the Virgin in Lourdes to Bernadette Soubiroux hallucinatory without denigrating them. We thereby mean: she actually *saw* with her eyes what other people could not see. The term passes no judgment on the truth or falsity of the vision. In fact, the question of truth does not occur on the level of sense perception. Whatever we perceive is "true to

our senses. *Truth* in the full sense exists only on the level
of judgment.

Yet sensory illumination need not be hallucinatory. It
need not even be mystical in the strict sense. In the exercises called "applications of the senses" Ignatius invites
the spiritual exercitant to see with his eyes what is
happening in the stable at Bethlehem, to hear the words
that are spoken, to smell and taste the sweetness of God,
to kiss the holy places where God is present. I doubt
whether a novice in spiritual life can do justice to those
exercises. Yet they were not intended for mystics only
and continue a long, mainly Franciscan tradition. Here
again the mystic builds on the foundation of ordinary
Christian piety. On the level of the imagination, other
forms of illumination take place. Saint John of the Cross
refers to the infused, passive states that affect the imagination as visions, revelations, voices and spiritual feelings. In these clearly mystical states, the person sees visions or hears words while remaining fully conscious of
their "imaginary," that is, nonsensuous character.
Teresa clearly distinguishes between sensory visions and
those visions which she "sees" without eyes. In general,
mystics do not rank visions, imaginary or sensory,
among the higher forms of divine illumination. Long
before our present knowledge of the unconscious they
easily suspected in these more dramatic phenomena of
altered consciousness illusions of the devil and hence
confronted all such visions with a critical mind. Only
their practical effects would reveal whether they came
from God or not. Our more advanced knowledge of the
unconscious has rendered us even more hesitant (perhaps too much!) to accept visions and voices as direct
expressions of God. Not surprisingly, when the soul is

shaken in its nether depths by the mystical alteration, archaic forms and types, barely veiled in the accepted symbols of the mystic's faith, will emerge to the surface. This is true in Zen Buddhism as well as in Christianity. There are good reasons to distrust any religious vision—hallucinatory or imaginary—that is not solidly anchored in an overall religious context. Even to visions which illuminate, rather than deceive, we should not attach any importance, Saint John of the Cross advises. In all circumstances it remains difficult to distinguish the epiphenomena of an unconscious transformation from an authentic divine illumination.

At best sensory and imaginary visions or voices play a supporting role in the mystical development. They may strengthen or concretize a mystical insight. Teresa's *Autobiography* provides an interesting example of this. At one point she describes a mystical contemplation of the Holy Spirit that was accompanied by an imaginary vision. The former belongs to the order of what mystics call dark contemplation or intellectual vision which provides no concrete elements, but only abstract relations. Saint Teresa describes the accompanying vision of the imagination as follows: "While in this condition I saw a dove over my head, very different from those we see on earth, for it had no feathers like theirs. Its wings were made of little shells which emitted a great brilliance . . . . It was larger than a dove. I seemed to hear the rustling of its wings. It must have been fluttering like this for the space of an Ave Maria. But my soul was in such a state that as it became lost in itself it also lost sight of the dove."[4] Because of their connection with higher forms of contemplation, Teresa, in spite of the suspicion with which she regards imaginary visions, considers them, when they are critically accepted, graces from which the soul may derive considerable spiritual benefit.

Let us now consider the highest forms of mystical illumination, the dark contemplation which, often in an instant, transforms the soul and fills it with lasting insight. I shall relate four such "visions" taken from different authors. The first is a succinct report that appears in the biography of Balthasar Alvarez, the one-time confessor of Saint Teresa and one of the most articulate mystics of the Spanish school. "Having placed myself in prayer I felt that God was there. I saw Him neither with my bodily eyes, nor through my imagination. Nevertheless, His presence was certain to me, and the sight I had of it was far more powerful than that of the imagination or of the corporeal eyes."[5]

In the Seventy-Fourth Sermon on the *Song of Songs*, Saint Bernard synthesizes a number of such experiences.

> Though He has frequently entered into my soul, I have never at any time been sensible of the precise moment of His coming. I have felt that He was present, I remember that He has been with me; I have sometimes been able even to have a presentiment that He would come: but never to feel His coming nor His departure. For whence He came to enter my soul, or whither He went on quitting it, by what means He has made entrance or departure, I confess that I know not even to this day . . . . It is not by the eyes that He enters, for He is without form or color that they can discern; nor by the ears, for His coming is without sound; nor by the nostrils, for it is not with the air, but with the mind that He is blended . . . . By what avenue then has He entered? Or perhaps the fact may be that He

has not entered at all, nor indeed come at all from outside: for not one of these things belongs to the outside. Yet, It has not come from within me, for it is good and I know that in me dwells no good thing. I have ascended higher than myself, and lo! I have found the Word above me still. My curiosity has led me to descend below myself also and yet I found Him still at a lower depth. If I have looked within myself I have found that He is beyond that which is outside of me; and if within, He was at an inner depth still."[6]

Among several others Teresa of Avila reports a Trinitarian vision, perhaps the most common among intellectual visions: "I once had such great light from that Presence of the Three Persons which I bear in my soul that it was impossible for me to doubt that the true and living God was present, and then I came to understand things which I shall never be able to describe. One of those was how human flesh was taken by the Person of the Son and not by other Persons."[7]

Yet I must confess that no narrative of a mystical illumination has moved me more by its ring of simple authenticity than the intellectual vision which Ignatius of Loyola received while at the stream at Manresa:

As he sat there the eyes of his understanding began to open. Without having any vision he understood —knew—many matters both spiritual and pertaining to the realm of letters. And that with such clearness that they seemed utterly new to him. There is no possibility of setting out in detail everything he then understood. The most that he can say is that he was given so great an enlightening of his mind that if one were to put together all the helps he has received from God and all other

> things that he has ever learned, they would not be
> the equal of what he received in that single illumi-
> nation. He was left with his understanding so en-
> lightened that he seemed to be another man with
> another mind than the one that was his before.[8]

Here we are confronted with the kind of intellectual vision of which even the cautious John of the Cross says
that no illusions can deceive the visionary. In these four
cases we are clearly in the realm of what John of the
Cross calls "dark contemplation." Dark, because no distinct "vision" occurs. There is nothing to be seen,
smelled, or heard as in the distinct visions of sense or
imagination.

Purely senseless, imaginationless illuminations of this
nature have also been called "intellectual visions." Yet
they are neither "visions" nor "intellectual." The term
intellectual here stands for *purely mental*, as opposed to
sensory or imaginary. It implies no kind of discursive
understanding.

In the second book of *The Dark Night of the Soul* (especially in chapters four through eight), John of the
Cross analyzes these highest states of infused contemplation. He refers to them as an inflowing of God into
the soul. At this height of awareness the mind's normal
powers of cognition no longer function. In the *night* of
the active powers of the mind, illumination means utter
darkness. Saint Teresa refers to the "ligature of the faculties" while God makes His presence felt "in the most
secret region of the soul, which has but a slight knowledge of it."

Teresa emphasizes the *unitive* aspect of the ultimate
mystical experience over the cognitive one. John of the
Cross describes it more in the language of illumination.

Yet in the Prologue to *The Ascent of Mount Carmel* he clearly combines the illumination with a union in love —"this dark night through which the soul passes in order to attain to the divine *light* of the perfect *union* of the love of God." The highest "intellectual" visions, he teaches, cannot be clearly seen by the understanding, but "they can nevertheless be felt in the substance of the soul with the sweetest touches and unions" (*Ascent* II, 24, 4). The supreme illumination, to the understanding no more than "a ray of darkness," has its deepest impact in the center of affection—the will. Only with its volitional function does the mind respond to the divine touch. Nevertheless Saint John continues to refer to the infused contemplation as a "passive understanding." Quite clearly the usual distinction between the cognitive and affective "faculties" no longer applies when all functions of the mind become united in a passive state that is both illuminating and unitive. John of the Cross insists that this union takes place "in the substance of the soul"—that is, at a point below that where the mind breaks open into a variety of functions. When divine reality touches the soul it bypasses the ordinary operations which are unfit to receive it. It directly reaches the source ("substance") of these operations. Saint Teresa likewise writes about that stage of the interior life at which the mystical grace has definitively broken through, that neither imagination nor memory nor understanding can be an obstacle to the divine blessings. At that point, "His Majesty is in such close contact and union with the *essence* of the soul" that nothing can disturb His presence (*The Interior Castle*, "Fifth Mansion" Ch. I).

Once the soul has reached this highest mystical

awareness, the distinction between ordinary states of consciousness and transitory, mystical states, so clear at earlier stages, recedes without vanishing completely. There still occur flashes of special illumination, but the general condition of the mystic has become "illuminated." Not that he or she is constantly in a state of trance! But he or she may often enter effortlessly into another world merely by closing the eyes. Even while occupying himself with daily tasks, the mystic in this state retains in the background of his mind the persistent awareness of God's presence. His consciousness has become transformed so as to allow him to live on two levels at once. At the surface the mystic is fully involved with the ordinary occupations and relations demanded by economic conditions and social status. But below the surface he or she constantly hears the *obligato* of the divine music. One does not distract from the other. On the contrary, the deeper layer of existence supports the shallower one and provides it with a broader base of meaning. Such mystics as Ignatius and Teresa who lived their later years in this state of mind became more efficient as their work became infused with a mystical inspiration.

Because of the permanent character of the highest state of contemplation, Saint Teresa and other mystics refer to it as a "marriage," that is a *state* of experience, rather than a singular experience. At this level God unites Himself with the soul in such a way that they become "like two who cannot be separated from one another."

Although the light which accompanies it may not be so clear, the soul is always aware that it is expe-

riencing this companionship. We might compare
the soul to a person who is with others in a very
bright room; and then suppose that the shutters
are closed so that the people are all in darkness.
The light by which they can be seen has been taken
away, and, until it comes back, we shall be unable
to see them, yet we are nonetheless aware that they
are there.[9]

In the preceding states the soul is frequently separated
from God's experienced presence. In the mystical marriage it becomes entirely and permanently submerged
by this presence.

At the beginning of the seventh mansion of her *Interior Castle* in which she will discuss the intellectual visions and the subsequent permanent union of the mystical marriage, Saint Teresa explains: "O great God!
Surely a creature as miserable as I must tremble to treat
of anything so far beyond what I deserve to understand." What more can I say about a subject so far beyond what I actually understand?

Conclusion

In the doctrine of sanctifying grace Christian theologians have consistently referred to the uncreated presence of God in the soul. Is it surprising that to this unique presence corresponds an equally unique experience? The Greek Fathers first conceived this presence as an *image* of God in the soul. An image, as they understood it, is by no means an external copy, but an active participation in the divine life. Active and progressive! But also passive and experiential. Spiritual life, then, consists in a never-ceasing process of assimilation to this divine presence in the soul, or, as Ruusbroec formulated it, a *growing toward the Image*.

The active process as well as the passive experience are unique, in that they are more fundamental than any other activity or form of awareness. But they are not *exclusive*, reserved to a spiritual elite. The divine presence, and even more the passive experience of that presence, remain a *privilege*, since all approximation to God belongs, by its very nature, to the order of grace. But life in grace, far from being exceptional, defines the very nature of Christian existence. If grace is not the exclusive privilege of the few, then neither is the experience of grace. A one-sided elitism has unfortunately marked the development of spiritual life in the West. Perhaps in reaction against the increasing worldliness of our culture, it more and more adopted the form of an exclusive and highly introspective cult at the periphery of the communal Christian life. In contrast to the Christian mysticism of the Eastern Church, Western spirituality suffers from a certain esoterism. It often appears a-sacramental, a-liturgical and not always sufficiently disposed to involve itself with the sanctification of the entire human community or even of the neighbor next door. All too often it has been inclined to withdraw from a society that held spiritual life in such low esteem and to turn instead inside the self. Not only the fifteenth-century *Imitation of Christ*, but many spiritual Christians in the ages after Thomas à Kempis have adopted Seneca's word as an adage of spiritual life as such: "Quoties inter homines fui, minus homo redii"— "As often I went among men, I returned less human."

Hence a complete picture of Christian spirituality includes more, and often quite different, attitudes than the ones we find in those to whom we have come to restrict the name "mystics." Those who have devoted their lives to works of Christian charity or to the public cult of God in the liturgy will be particularly sensitive to this historical one-sidedness. In leading spiritual lives they will feel the need to return to the sources of Christian mysticism, the Scriptures and the Greek Fathers, to compensate for a later, all too exclusive emphasis on inwardness. Nevertheless, Western men and women are struggling with the same problems that confronted the mystics in our culture. Being all too inclined, like our secular contemporaries, to reduce life, including spiritual life, to a soulless objectivity, we cannot but profit from the spiritual message of those who, exposed to similar temptations, vigorously asserted the primacy of the divine life in us.

In doing so we shall meet spiritual men and women of other times, other cultures, other faiths. Christian theology provides no ground for dismissing the experienced presence of God in nonChristians. If grace is not restricted to Christians, neither is the experience of grace. In the preceding lectures I have insisted on respecting the *specific* character of a particular mystical tradition, and never to assume that mystics, in different theological jargons, express the same truth. The different language indicates a different experience of the divine presence. Yet after having so strongly stressed the diversity of the mystical experience, we must conclude by appreciating the underlying unity. The experiences are not identical, but the dimension of consciousness in which the various experiences occur is—a dimension far removed from our ordinary states of being in the world. This common dimension conveys to all spiritual men and women a family resemblance that allows them to consider each other brothers and sisters in the Spirit.

Notes

Chapter 1
1. Richard Jeffries, *The Story of My Heart* (London: Duckworth, 1912), p. 3.

Chapter 2
1. St. Augustine, *Confessions*, trans. Pusey (The Book League of America, 1936).

Chapter 3
1. Pseudo-Dionysius, *The Mystical Theology*, Migne P. G. 3, 997.
2. *Meister Eckhart*, trans. R. B. Blakney (New York: Harper & Row, Torchbooks, 1957), pp. 59–60.
3. *Ibid.*, p. 205.
4. *Ibid.*, p. 181.
5. *Ibid.*, p. 228.
6. *Ibid.*, p. 226.

Chapter 4
1. *Meister Eckhart*, trans. R. B. Blakney (New York: Harper & Row, Torchbooks, 1957), p. 228.
2. *Ibid.*, p. 229.

Chapter 5
1. Jan Ruusbroec, *The Adornment of the Spiritual Marriage*, trans. Dom C. A. Wynschenck (Philadelphia: Westminster Press, Christian Classics, 1974).

92 · *The Deeper Life*

2. *Ibid.*, p. 172.
3. Author unknown, hymn from Gethsemani Abbey.

Chapter 6
1. St. John of the Cross, *The Ascent of Mount Carmel*, I, 13 (New York: Doubleday, Image Books, 1958).
2. St. Ignatius of Loyola, *The Spiritual Exercises*, trans. Louis J. Puhl, S.J. (New York: The Newman Press, 1954), p. 69.

Chapter 8
1. St. John of the Cross, *The Ascent of Mount Carmel*, I, 6 (New York: Doubleday, Image Books, 1958).
2. *Ibid.*, I, 13.
3. *Ibid.*
4. St. John of the Cross, *The Dark Night of the Soul*, I, 8 (New York: Doubleday, Image Books, 1959).
5. *Ibid.*
6. St. Catherine of Siena, *The Divine Dialogue*, trans. Algar Thorold, 1926.

Chapter 9
1. Evelyn Underhill, *Mysticism* (New York: Dutton, 1961), p. 300.
2. Cf. Ronald Knox, *Enthusiasm*, p. 291.
3. St. Teresa of Avila, *The Interior Castle*, Fourth Mansion (New York: Doubleday, 1961), p. 85.
4. _____ , *Life*, trans. Allison Peers in *Works* I, p. 271.
5. Louis Du Pont, *The Life of Fr. Balthasar Alvarez* (1868), p. 171.
6. St. Bernard, Sermon 74 on *Song of Songs*, trans. Evelyn Underhill in *Mysticism* (New York: Dutton, 1961), p. 244.
7. St. Teresa of Avila, *Relations*, trans. Allison Peers in *Works* I, p. 362.
8. St. Ignatius of Loyola, *Autobiography*, trans. Elmer O'Brien in *Varieties of Mystical Experience*, p. 246–7.
9. St. Teresa of Avila, *The Interior Castle*, Seventh Mansion, p. 211.